GREENS

Poems by Arnold Adoff

Illustrated by Betsy Lewin

Lothrop, Lee & Shepard Books   New York

KERMIT THE FROG is a trademark of Henson Associates, Inc., and is used in this book by permission.

Text copyright © 1988 by Arnold Adoff
Illustrations copyright © 1988 by Betsy Lewin
All rights reserved. No part of this book may be reproduced or utilized in any form or by any means, electronic or mechanical, including photocopying, recording or by any information storage and retrieval system, without permission in writing from the Publisher. Inquiries should be addressed to Lothrop, Lee & Shepard Books, a division of William Morrow & Company, Inc., 105 Madison Avenue, New York, New York 10016. Printed in the United States of America.

First Edition 1 2 3 4 5 6 7 8 9 10

Library of Congress Cataloging in Publication Data
Adoff, Arnold. Greens.
Summary: Illustrated poems about the color green. 1. Green — Juvenile poetry. 2. Children's poetry, American. [1. Green — Poetry. 2. American poetry] I. Lewin, Betsy, ill. II. Title. PS3551.D66G7 1987 811'.54
85-16631
ISBN 0-688-04276-7   ISBN 0-688-04277-5 (lib. bdg.)

For
Ker
Mit
The
    Frog
    With
    This
    Kiss
And
Hug
For
    Being
    Green
And
For
His
    Green Song

    Live Long

Green kite in March breeze
                     Diving
        Into
           March   trees
Just
Beginning to
         Bud
Green

Hold tight
        And this
            Thin white
                String
Will
Pull you into the
           Next   season
Will
Pull you into
            A
Green Spring

In The Heavy Spring Breeze

The green leaves   the hundreds
                              Of
      Green leaves
                    Each a different shade
Flash
      And
Turn
Like hundreds of green tops
                          Spinning
Like hundreds of green tops
            Along the top of the cottonwood tree

They are greeting the new season
                        Spinning into Spring
            Greeting me
Just
Made for me

9

Caterpillar to the leaf
Leaf to the stem of the leaf
Stem of the leaf
To the twig
Twig
To the branch
Branch
To the trunk
Trunk

Trunk of the tree
In
To the
Green
Ground
Of
Spring

As Soon As She Is Up

Grandma is up
        And
        Out   side
Picking the
Fresh
        And
          New
        And
        Tender

        Dandelion greens   to
                    Cook
                    Up
                    For
                    Us
                    All

All Day Long

    Green
    Grass hoppers hop
           High
    Fly by
      My
    Feet   in the high grass

    Instant replay
        And
      Repeat

    Green
    Grass hoppers hop
           High

Fly by
　　My
　　Feet　in the high grass
　　　　　　And
　　　　Repeat

　　All day long
　　　　Song

Grass

Green and
Greener
    Than
Green
    A
Thousand
Shades in the noon
        Day
        Sun
          Un
          Der
My running feet

O
Grass
O
Grass
O
Green
Grass
Wr_{in}kl_{in}g
Under my feet

I know the next
Shower
Will
S t r a i g h t e n you out

I want to grow
That
S
t
r
a
i
g
h
t
That
Fast

                    Under the hottest Summer sun
Green garden hose
Is
My shower
            Fills
My pool
            Keeps
Me cool
    And
    Waters the dusty flowers   I planted in the
                                    Spring

Green garden hose
Is the best thing
            Under the hottest Summer sun
                                    Is
                                    The
                                    Most fun

Summer Leaves

               Are
               At their brightest
                   Green
On the bushes
             Outside   my window
             But
It
Is the
   Red berries that bring
      The hungry birds

Momma Drives

        This
        Pick
        Up
Truck
        Full of
Newspapers
            To
The
    Re
    Cycle
    Center   and I help carry
               The bags inside

Momma drives and I am along
                    To work
And
For the good talk
   This good ride

Green Truck

Stuck
In brown
Mud

Tan
Woman
With
Red face
Kicks
Gray
Stone
Kicks
Green
Truck

We walk
Back
To our
Place
Talking
About
Bad luck

19

In The Fall After The First Frost

All
The trees will turn
Their Autumn shades of
Tan
And
Red
And gold and brown

Yellow

But green hides
Under
Snow
Until
Spring

The
Old
Tin
   Roof
      Of
The
   House   is a bright green thing
                Showing
                      The promise of
                             Next
                             Spring

Through the
                Snowing

Afternoon

Ever
Greens

    Are
Darkest
Green are
Almost
Black
Against   the
    White snow
       And
       The bright blue sky
           Shows
       Cold and still
       In the winter after
           Noon

We stay
    Back
We play   inside by the fire

In My Coloring Book

This green van
                    With
        This green man
From   far
Beyond Mars
From
Beyond   our
                Stars   is   driving   down
                        My PaperAndCrayons
                                    Street

He
  Says he wants to meet   my   mother
But
                She is looking the other way
                                    And

He cannot stay
For the next
            Page

23

One night   Kermit The Frog was riding along
              On the back
              Of the Loch
                    Ness Monster
              Through
                    The waters of the Hudson
                                        River
On their way out to sea
                To the
Atlantic Ocean
And back to Scotland
                Kermit was singing his   special
                                            Song
                And the Loch Ness Monster Was
                                            Wag
                                               g
                                               i
                                               n
                                               g
His great
        Green tail along   just right

        I know they were happy in the night

24

From the dark
        Green
        Atlantic
      Deep
One
    Flashing
      Blue
And white
      Fin
One
    Swordfish
      Fin
      Cutting

    The green water
        Like
A moving knife

      Leaping
      In

Turtle

        Will not hurtle
Turtle
     Will not   leap
Turtle
     Will c r a w l
        S l o w l y
Turtle
     Will
     Dive
     Deep

Turtle

I am tired of coloring green
                            Grass
                            Green
And red
            Apples
        Red
        And faces pink and brown

        Yellow hair on a
                    Tan round
                            Head
        Or another red nose on a
                            White
                            Face
                            Clown

I want a red lawn instead of green
And an orange banana a purple frog
                        On a purple log
                            And
A tasty black green bean

I want a green woman and a green man
With all our faces colored the same
                    In this green
                            Game

A Green Monster Face

Is staring from the
                    M i d d l e
Of my split pea soup
Is
Not
        Scaring me with
                        His
        Split pea eye
                        His
        Split pea grin

I dip my spoon right
                    In
And race him   to
                    The
            B o t t o m
Of the bowl

He disappears without a trace
                            And
The split pea grin
                Is on my face

28

Greens to the left
                Of
                Me
Greens to the
                Right
Greens are climbing
                Up
                My
                Fork
                So
Momma
        Now I bite

Beans
    To the north
          Of
          Me
Beans
    To the   south

Beans
    Are
Leaning   on my chin
    Are
Sliding   in my
         Mouth

GREEN SKIRT
GREEN HAT

GREEN SHIRT
        THE
        SAME

        WITH
ORANGE
LETTERS
        THAT
    PROCLAIM

NOTRE   DAME

31

At Christmas Time I Open My Banks

And pile my nickles
            Quarters
                  Dimes   to spend for
                                   Presents
                                         And
                                   There is
                                   Always a
                                   Little extra
                                   To lend my
                                         Sister
                                   Interest
                                         Free

For me
A low hill of wrinkled dollar bills
That will buy my dad this shirt
                              That
            Will buy my mom this green
                                   Plant

At Christmas time   I open my banks
And change my money into thanks

32

Greta

This
Baby
Sister
Girl
Has
Really
Green
Eyes
That
Shine
Into
Mine

Such
Fine
Eyes
Such
Fine
Family
Eyes

Greens

Pistachio ice cream   grass   trees   leaves   Jell-O
          My best green jacket lying in the snow
                    And   smelly   cheese

Lettuce
Cabbage   all the parts of a grasshopper
                    Standing very still
          The green
                    Blur   of a grasshopper
                              Hopp
                                ing
          Down my best green hill
                    And green peas

Beautiful broccoli   awful sour apples   a sweet plum
                    And under this thumb
My green pen writing green
                    Words that please and rhyme
                    And mean I am doing my best

All the rest   is other colors   for   another   time

Arnold Adoff

believes that "writing a poem is making music with words and space," and that *Greens* is "a young book, full of music and rhythm and *much rhyme*." He was born and educated in New York City and has been writing "some kind of poetry" since adolescence. Now a noted author, poet, and anthologist, he has published fifteen books of poetry, including ALA Notables *Eats* and *All the Colors of the Race*, for Lothrop. Mr. Adoff and his wife, the author Virginia Hamilton, are Distinguished Visiting Professors at Queens College in New York City.

Betsy Lewin's

charming illustrations have appeared in *Furlie Cat* by Berniece Freschet and *Penny* by Beatrice Schenk de Regniers. The artist lives in Brooklyn, New York.